1950s

Fashion

Coloring Book for Girls

This Book belongs to :

_____

MEZZO ZENTANGLE DESIGNS

MEZZO
ZENTANGLE
DESIGNS

MEZZO
ZENTANGLE
DESIGNS

MEZZO
ZENTANGLE
DESIGNS

MEZZO
ZENTANGLE
DESIGNS

MEZZO
ZENTANGLE
DESIGNS

MEZZO
ZENTANGLE
DESIGNS

MEZZO
ZENTANGLE
DESIGNS

MEZZO
ZENTANGLE
DESIGNS

MEZZO
ZENTANGLE
DESIGNS

MEZZO
ZENTANGLE
DESIGNS

MEZZO
ZENTANGLE
DESIGNS

MEZZO
ZENTANGLE
DESIGNS

MEZZO
ZENTANGLE
DESIGNS

MEZZO
ZENTANGLE
DESIGNS

MEZZO
ZENTANGLE
DESIGNS

MEZZO
ZENTANGLE
DESIGNS

MEZZO
ZENTANGLE
DESIGNS

MEZZO
ZENTANGLE
DESIGNS

MEZZO
ZENTANGLE
DESIGNS

MEZZO
ZENTANGLE
DESIGNS

MEZZO
ZENTANGLE
DESIGNS

MEZZO
ZENTANGLE
DESIGNS

MEZZO
ZENTANGLE
DESIGNS

MEZZO
ZENTANGLE
DESIGNS

MEZZO
ZENTANGLE
DESIGNS

MEZZO
ZENTANGLE
DESIGNS

MEZZO
ZENTANGLE
DESIGNS

MEZZO
ZENTANGLE
DESIGNS

MEZZO
ZENTANGLE
DESIGNS

MEZZO
ZENTANGLE
DESIGNS

MEZZO
ZENTANGLE
DESIGNS

MEZZO
ZENTANGLE
DESIGNS

MEZZO
ZENTANGLE
DESIGNS

MEZZO
ZENTANGLE
DESIGNS

MEZZO
ZENTANGLE
DESIGNS

MEZZO
ZENTANGLE
DESIGNS

MEZZO
ZENTANGLE
DESIGNS

MEZZO
ZENTANGLE
DESIGNS

MEZZO
ZENTANGLE
DESIGNS

MEZZO
ZENTANGLE
DESIGNS

MEZZO
ZENTANGLE
DESIGNS

MEZZO
ZENTANGLE
DESIGNS

MEZZO
ZENTANGLE
DESIGNS

MEZZO
ZENTANGLE
DESIGNS

MEZZO
ZENTANGLE
DESIGNS

MEZZO
ZENTANGLE
DESIGNS

MEZZO
ZENTANGLE
DESIGNS

Made in the USA
Coppell, TX
05 November 2024

39657384R00057